GW00984540

The
Mass Explained

by
Fr Charles Dilke

*All booklets are published thanks to the
generous support of the members of the
Catholic Truth Society*

CATHOLIC TRUTH SOCIETY
PUBLISHERS TO THE HOLY SEE

Contents

Preface

The material in this booklet was originally given as some talks to the members of the Catholic Evidence Guild in 1993 on the subject of misgivings aroused by modern changes in the Roman Mass. It was reviewed and revised in 2007. I must state at once that they represent no claim on my part to be a liturgical scholar, only a student of history. In general I have used as material the works of Archdale King, Jungmann and the collection of Documents on the Liturgy 1963-1979.

The Brompton Oratory
5th December 2007

Introduction

It is obviously undesirable to give the impression that the Roman liturgy is the whole liturgy or the only important liturgy, but the history of the liturgy is so vast that it seems better to concentrate on how it looks from one centre rather than try and cover so many different nations and cultures as have developed particular liturgical traditions. Another reason for making this study of the Roman rite lies in the fact that there are quite a few devout people who feel, either explicitly or as it were by instinct that the so-called "Tridentine Mass" has an authenticity about it which is lacking in the Mass we celebrate today, namely the Paul VI Mass or Vatican II Mass. These people make us all ask ourselves - has the Mass changed in some essential way, or has the holiness of our Mass become less than it was before Vatican II? A strong unease or even a vague unease about the most important act of our religion is highly undesirable in the Church and for the individuals. The question needs to be settled one way or another. And it seems to me and to others whom I have consulted that what is required is a reasonably thorough and of course accurate examination of how in fact the Church has celebrated Mass in the course of her long history. By seeing what has been done by the saints and often less-than-saints of old, people like ourselves as far as human nature and grace are concerned, perhaps we may see clearer the nature of the Mass and so be able to judge for ourselves and maybe for others whom we talk to, the changes that have taken place in the Mass of our own time.

However I don't want to foster any false "archaeologism", as though the past is to be returned to as a golden age. It is much more a matter of going into a well furnished room and making an inventory of the contents. We can only make an estimate of the value if we have a reasonably accurate overview. So it is to be rather like a guided tour of the Holy Mass, if this doesn't seem too irreverent. When you go on a guided tour of a country house, for example, what you want from the guide is not a personal interpretation but someone who can open the right doors, give essential information and allow you to make your own assessment and your own appreciation. Accordingly the booklet contains three parts. This first deals with the Growth of the Roman Rite. Next, the Reform of the Roman Rite. And in the final chapter I shall try and gather the threads together to bring about an understanding of the modern changes of our own time.

The Primitive Roman Mass

The Canon

Let us begin by trying to see what Mass would have been like the first time it was said in Rome. Later in time, some people, even Popes, would say that, for example, the Roman Canon (Canon No. 1) was composed by St Peter himself and has never been subsequently changed. An examination of the available documents however shows clearly that this was not the case. The Roman Canon was probably composed in more or less its present form about 350 AD and after that some of what is now in the Canon, for example the commemoration of the Dead, had to wait several centuries before being inserted into the Canon of the Mass. So we find that for over three hundred years, Mass was celebrated without the benefit of the Roman Canon. Was it therefore the same Mass? Evidently it was, since there is absolutely no record or trace of any sense of discontinuity, any idea that something new was being done when eventually the Roman Canon took shape. The statement by saints and doctors that some rite or prayer, such as the Roman Canon, goes back to the apostles, has therefore to be taken in the sense that the essence of the prayer or rite indeed goes back to the apostles but this cannot be said for the particular form of words.

Additions and Subtractions

In the course of time many features have been added to the Mass but we must also remember that features have also been subtracted from it. And quite often features have been added, then subtracted and then added again. For example incense was used in the Jewish Liturgy and the Apocalypse contains a vision of the heavenly court that shows incense being used freely. But in the following century incense does not seem to have been used because by then the big persecutions and battle with imperial paganism had begun and incense had associations with the Imperial cult. The martyrs died rather than offer grains of incense on a pagan altar. But then, at the cessation of persecution in the 4th century, incense was once more introduced into the liturgy on the model of its use before dignitaries of state officiating in the civil basilicas or law-courts. Another example is Holy Communion on Good Friday, first practised, then strictly forbidden and then reintroduced. Quite often, too, people, even Popes and Bishops, have forgotten changes made by order of their predecessors and have thought that things have always been as they were in their own day. Thus, leavened bread was used from very early on, in spite of the use of unleavened bread at the Last Supper, until the latter was once again introduced at Rome in the 8th century. But by the 11th century people were saying that unleavened bread had always been used.

The First Masses

So then, what would Mass have been like when it was first celebrated in the city of Rome? There must have been Christians in Rome before either Peter or Paul arrived there as Acts records that proselytes from Rome heard the mighty acts of God proclaimed at Jerusalem on the Day of Pentecost. Some of them would have been baptised and then spread their new faith back home. Joined to the Mass there was a function which has long since died out. This was the *Agapé*, which was a Jewish type ceremonial meal with blessings and prayers. People brought their own food and as well as the blessings spoken by the senior ecclesiastic present there was conversation on matters important to the group. This was the sort of weekly meeting that a teacher would hold in Israel with his disciples and Our Lord would have done it with his followers. The Mass was celebrated, though the word Mass was not used until 300 years later. At this stage it was called *Klasis Artou*, Greek for the breaking of Bread.

Language

The language used may have been Aramaic at first but this would soon have been replaced by Greek as all Jews in Rome would have spoken Greek. Latin was spoken by the native inhabitants but we must remember that our Faith came to Rome as a foreign, eastern religion and few of the first Christians at Rome would have been native Romans. As foreigners the only common language among the Christians would have been Greek. It was not until about 300 AD that the Faith had sufficiently penetrated the native population to make it necessary to use Latin. Latin came into the Roman liturgy about the time Constantine made Christianity the official religion of the Empire. The Greek formulas and prayers were then translated into Latin, the opportunity being taken, to prune them of their more flowery Greek expressions. The texts of the Latin Rite have always been shorter, more prosaic, and less full of symbolism and mysticism than the texts of the Greek rites and the Eastern liturgies.

The Order of Mass

Apart from the *Agapé*, the Mass would begin at dawn. There would have been no Introductory rites, no *Confiteor*, no *Kyrie*, *Gloria* or Collect. The first thing would have been the continuous reading from the Old Testament, chosen from whatever scrolls the community might happen to possess. There would be comment and preaching from whoever was saying the Mass. He would be known as the Elder but it is possible he might have been a Prophet, one with the charismatic gift of speaking in the Name of the Lord. After this, according to St Justin who wrote in the middle of the 2nd century AD, there were Prayers, the Prayer of the Faithful or what we call Bidding Prayers. These remain a part of the Roman Mass until they died out in the 6th century AD. The probable cause of this was that by the time the Canon had so grown in length that it included in itself the petitions that previously had been made in the Prayer of the Faithful. There has always been a tendency to try and fit things into the Canon, as the holiest part of the Mass, the part where petitions would have been most efficacious. Having died out in the 6th century, the Prayer of the Faithful came back again with Vatican II in our own time, rather duplicating, it must be said, the Canon with all its petitions.

When the Prayer for the Faithful was finished the Kiss of Peace was given among all present. One must remember that men and women were, in the Jewish fashion, separated. The kiss was the normal greeting of the time, at least in religious circles, even outside the Mass, as we can see from the salutations in St Paul's Epistles. After the Prayer of the Faithful died out, the Kiss of Peace moved to its present position just before Communion. By the end of the Middle Ages it was exchanged only by the clergy but in England at least an attempt was made to continue it by using little tablets called Pax Tablets. (These are still in use at the exercises of the Brothers of the Little Oratory in London.)

After the Kiss, a white table cloth was laid with dignity and formality on a wooden table and bread, wine and water was placed on it. This was done without any ceremony for the first 200 years or so. Then it became quite solemn with the people bringing up gifts of food and wine, from which the *oblata* for the Mass were selected, so it took some time and a chant was sung. While we mention a chant, this might be the place to mention that singing and perhaps instruments would have been part of the Mass, when available, from the beginning, because the Jews were in the habit of chanting in the synagogues and the Temple. The first Christians would have used the same chants but quite soon replaced them with Greek chants, again adapting from what already existed in pagan Greek worship.

With or without chant, therefore, the gifts were placed, without any prayers or ritual, on the wooden table with its linen cloth, probably on glass patens and in a glass chalice. Wooden tables were replaced with stone ones in the 4th century and in the following century wooden ones were strictly forbidden. Glass for the sacred vessels continued to be used less and less until finally forbidden about 900 AD.

The celebrant then began the Canon or Eucharistic Prayer with the Dialogue which is probably the oldest formula of the Mass except for the words of consecration themselves. The prayers show ancient Semitic and Greek characteristics. After the dialogue he launched at once into what we call the Preface and the Canon. There was no distinction between the Preface and the Canon because there was no Sanctus, so that from the Dialogue until Amen at the end was one uninterrupted prayer. Moreover at the time we are speaking of, 1st century AD, there was no fixed form, still less any written form, for the prayer. Each Celebrant, though saying the same thing in substance, chose his own words. It is difficult to say whether it was much longer or much shorter than as now, probably both depending on the celebrant. The Sanctus was inserted into this one prayer just after the Roman Canon was fixed in its present, Latin, form. The Canon was said aloud until at least the 6th century, and in fact it was probably the insertion of the Sanctus which was the reason for the Canon beginning to be said silently. When choirs began to sing elaborate Sanctuses and Benedictuses, celebrants began to say the Canon silently and simultaneously with the Sanctus so as to prevent the Mass becoming too long. Vatican II ordered that the Canon once more be said aloud and therefore at a Solemn Mass the celebrant is supposed to wait until the choir has finished not only the Sanctus but also the Benedictus.

The Fraction

At the very early time we are speaking of there was a feature of the Canon which was quite different from now and which is something that so far from being an embellishment has in fact all but disappeared. This was the Fraction, the breaking of the host. This was such a distinctive feature of the Mass as said by the apostles that it gave its name to the whole liturgy, the Breaking of the Bread. It was done at the time of consecration, accompanying the words, "He took bread, broke it..." It was in fact the climax, ritually speaking, of the Mass, together with the Commixture that was done just before Communion, when some of the Host was mixed with the Precious Blood in the chalice. It was a relic of the Jewish custom at meals of mixing bread with wine, as illustrated in St John's Gospel in the text describing how Our Lord identified the traitor by giving him a morsel which he had dipped. The Fraction was considered of very great importance as a symbol of ecclesiastical unity and early on a rite developed whereby a morsel from the Pope's Mass was carried in procession to be dipped in the chalice at Masses said in the other churches of Rome. It was called the *Fermentum*.

As it took some time to break the large Hosts into small pieces for the Communion of the faithful, a chant and a concluding prayer was provided. Pope St Gregory the Great thought the Pater Noster, as our Lord's own prayer formula, ought to be said closer to the Consecration and so he ordered that it should be said before the Fraction. From then on the Fraction declined in importance until now when the priest could easily omit it without anyone noticing. Its history is a good example of how, due to quite understandable and practical reasons, different parts of the Mass have received emphasis or de-emphasis at different moments in the Church's history.

After the Conmixture, Communion was given and received in both kinds. The communicants stood in devout attitude and received in the hand and then the Mass was over, without concluding rites, prayers or final blessing of any kind, though probably a hymn was sung.

Growth and Enrichment of the Rites

Ceremonial & Vestments

Very quickly in the Roman rite a certain ceremonial was attached to the entry of the celebrant and ministers at the beginning of the Mass and again at the procession of the Gospel book, accompanied by incense, when the custom of reading an extract from the Gospel was introduced. Those two rites seem to have been the only places when there was any ceremonial in the early Roman Mass. The final thing to describe in this Mass is the attire of the ministers. There were no vestments at all, but they wore civil dress. At that time normal dress was a tunic, a belt and as your best garment, a dalmatic or sort of jacket. The tunic was called an alb, the belt became a girdle. You could wear an overcoat which was called a chasuble. Even in the 5th century Popes reproved clerics who tried to dress differently from laymen. But it was usual to keep one set for Mass only. What then happened was that in the era of barbarian infiltration, secular dress changed. The tunic was shortened into our shirt, trousers were introduced. Dalmatics and chasubles gave way to cloaks.

But while secular dress changed, no one liked to change the clothes worn by the clergy at Mass and so the divergence began between secular and liturgical dress. Once the divergence existed, then symbolism got to work and the various colours and distinctions of mediaeval vestments developed.

Time of Liturgical Revolution

You may have noticed that a lot of things began to change in the rite of Mass from the beginning of the 4th century until the time of Gregory the Great about 600 AD.

There was a sort of liturgical revolution due to a number of circumstances. The era of persecutions, at least by the pagan empire, ended, the cult of saints and martyrs grew enormously and the previously rather fluid and extempore and sometimes unorthodox forms of prayer were replaced by the more precise formulas drawn up by or under the aegis of a number of Popes of great administrative ability. All the great centres of Christian culture, Antioch, Alexandria, Constantinople, Africa, Gaul, Spain and of course Rome itself, began to form their own liturgical traditions. Rome discovered its own Latin language and administrative genius but for all that was still greatly influenced from the East. One can say that nearly all the symbolism and poetry in the Roman Mass came from the East, as did the best of its Christian

religious art. In the beginning the only feasts in the
Christian calendar were Easter and Pentecost. All the other
feasts came to Rome after being celebrated in the Eastern
Empire. Christmas may possibly be the one exception, and
of course the feasts, growing more and more important, of
Rome's own saints and martyrs. In the rite of Mass it was
now that the three prayers of the celebrant, the Collect,
Prayer over the Gifts and Post Communion were added. It
was now that the Old Testament reading was omitted and
a scheme of Gospel extracts for the whole year was
prepared. It was in these centuries that the Kyrie,
beginning as a long litany, imitating those used in the East,
and the Gloria, an ancient hymn for Morning Prayer,
became part of the Mass.

Charlemagne's Enrichments

At the same time as the Roman liturgy was being
organised and enriched and provided with fixed texts, so
also were the liturgies of the East and of Africa, France
and Spain. There was no feeling at all that everyone ought
to follow the Roman Rite. Occasionally the Popes,
conscious of their obligation to be concerned for all the
churches, intervened in a liturgical dispute, but this was
very rare. On the whole, they felt that churches founded
from Rome ought to follow Roman customs. This usually
happened, however, less because Rome insisted on it than

because other churches of their own accord wanted to adopt the Roman use. The greatest example of this and the cause of the next stage of the enrichment of the Roman Rite was Charlemagne, the first Western Emperor, crowned at Rome in 800. Throughout his dominions which covered France and Germany, he laboured to replace the native Galician rites with the Roman liturgy, but to this liturgy he also was responsible for adding many embellishments, aided by various able bishops and monks. Introductory Rites for Mass were begun but not accepted at Rome until the Middle Ages. Likewise the Creed was inserted and similarly resisted at Rome. It was contended that the purpose of introducing the Creed was to defend the Church against heresy but as Rome had never suffered any heretical beliefs there was no need to have the Creed in the Roman Mass. All this time, you see, the Roman Mass was the local liturgy of Rome. Nobody else was obliged to follow it.

After Charlemagne had adopted the Roman rite and embellished it, he then tried to export it so to speak back to Rome but Rome put up a stiff resistance. Only about 1000AD did Rome accept this enriched version of the Mass. It was from about that date that the Confiteor came into the Roman Mass, that the bringing of gifts to the altar by the people died out, that candles and ornaments began to be permitted to appear on the altar itself instead of being somewhere near it and that the Creed came in. The adoption of prayers at the Offertory did not take place at Rome till the 13th century. It was also at this time that Communion under two kinds died out, though efforts continued to be made, in England and elsewhere, to provide some substitute for the chalice, for example, the use of intinction or the giving of unconsecrated wine to the laity. The Elevation of the Host, then the Chalice, at the consecration was only popularised about 1200 and became the climax of the Mass for the people, just as the Fraction had been at the beginning.

The Spread of the Roman Rite

In all this Rome displayed a great reluctance to change, trying as hard as possible to keep its character of a local Church. This attempt finally ended when the Franciscan Order, in its pristine vigour, adopted the Missal and Office book provided by Rome for use by curial officials, with everything conveniently and slightly more shortly provided in one book. The Franciscans made some alterations and the resulting liturgy was adopted by Rome as its own and the distribution of the Franciscans spread it more and more throughout the Church. Thus it was in the late Middle Ages that the Roman Mass lost most of its character of local Romanness and became a Rite which competed with and finally replaced the rites of the various regions of the Church, such as the Sarum used in England. However in the Middle Ages right up to the Reformation period local diocesan rites and the rites of religious orders flourished richly and many embellishments and extra prayers of all kinds were introduced into the Mass.

These new prayers and rites were accepted after some time by Rome and became part of the rite as written down in Missals. In this way the Last Gospel was introduced as a thanksgiving, as were the customs of the priest kissing the altar before and after turning his back on it to address the faithful and the signs of the cross made during the Canon of the Mass, to sacralise all references to the *oblata* in the text, and the genuflections at various points in the Mass. All of these came into being during the later Middle Ages and became standardised only when the reformed Missal was produced by St Pius V in 1570. And this mention of "reform" brings us to the next stage of liturgical history - after the age of growth, we now come to consider the age of reform.

Reform of the Mass

Ongoing Reform

Up to now we have been considering the growth and enrichment of the Roman Mass. As we now turn to consider the reform of its liturgy we must avoid giving the impression that an age of enrichment, say, up to the end of the Middle Ages, was followed by an age of reform. Although "reform" in and of the Church was being increasingly demanded as the Middle Ages advanced, yet from the point of view of the liturgy, "reform" was something that had already happened many times already, long before either the Reformation or the Counter-Reformation movements of the 16th century. You will have realised that change has been taking place in the rites of the Mass practically all the time ever since it was instituted and often this change took the form of "reform". For example, we have seen how the era of extempore and variable prayers which prevailed in the first 3 centuries of the Church came to an end with the organisation of fixed liturgical forms centred on the major urban centres of Christian life. This was really a work of reform, an effort to eliminate unorthodox texts and unsuitable liturgical practices. Popes like Damasus, Leo and Gregory were liturgical reformers. In the same way some centuries later, Charlemagne carried out a major work of liturgical reform in the territories over which he ruled, a reform which spread into other territories as well, such as Rome or England. And again mediaeval Popes like Innocent III were reformers putting order into the customs of the Papal Chapel and hoping that this would serve as an example and pattern for other churches to follow.

So there is no question of there ever having been an age of no liturgical change, no efforts to reform. But at the Reformation there did begin an age when "reform" itself took on a kind of life of its own. Its starting point was the need to eliminate the many overgrown enrichments of the liturgy which took place in the mediaeval period, leading to widespread abuses and superstitions. As in ancient times, so also in the Middle Ages, the celebration of Mass was directed not by Rome or by texts authorised by Rome, but by the Bishops and the leaders of religious orders. Often there was present in people's minds a desire to "return" to the ancient and simple forms of the Roman liturgy but local bishops and abbots were also confidently sure that they knew how to adapt the rite to the traditions of their peoples and indeed to improve and enrich it in ways that made greater impact on people of the time. This state of affairs might have continued had not the need for more thorough reform become increasingly evident.

The Reformation

Due to development in society, the Great Schism, the Black Death, the growth of urbanism, it became impossible for any one bishop however zealous to conduct a reforming crusade against the many evils resulting from avarice and superstition and sheer ignorance. Something needed to be done from the centre. The things that needed correcting in the liturgy were not just local and sporadic abuses but were widespread customs incorporated into the social and economic life of society. Some idea of what they were can be gained from a study of the decrees of the Council of Trent which eventually made the long-desired reforms. Mass was being said by ignorant chantry priests who did not know Latin, gross superstitions about the number of candles to be lit, or the numbers of sequences of Masses to be said in order to produce infallibly some desired answer to prayer. Mass was being said at street corners, in bedrooms for newly married couples, and other unsuitable places. Extravagant things were said to encourage people to have Masses said and attributed to the Fathers of the Church, for example that one did not grow old while one was hearing Mass, a maxim attributed to St Augustine.

The Fathers of the Council of Trent also criticised the many Prefaces containing unhistorical legends, the offertory prayers and the large number of signs of the cross making it seem that the bread and wine were consecrated before the words of Institution. They wished to reform the avarice of the clergy in search of Mass stipends (without which many of them would have starved), the saying of Mass without servers or anyone present, the use of extravagant gestures during the celebration, the behaviour of the people attending Mass, to stop them using Mass as any occasion of doing business, hearing the news and chatting to friends.

The Council of Trent

Luther and his followers decided that the only way to rid the Church of these abuses was to declare that the Mass would only help in our salvation if it increased the Faith that justifies - of itself it had no effect. Hence the Council of Trent began by stating in positive terms the doctrine of the Mass before passing on to lay down a programme for the reform of abuses. Basically it was a two-point programme, firstly to educate the clergy and improve their life-style by training them in seminaries and secondly to make use of the recent invention of printing to produce liturgical texts which were to be imposed uniformly over the whole Western Church with full papal authority. The Pope was asked by the Council to take this work in hand and issue new and standard editions of the Missal and the Breviary.

Thus it was that the so-called Tridentine Mass came into being. St Pius V found himself confronted with a task that no one had ever had to do in the Church, to produce a standard text for Mass for use everywhere in the Latin rite. It was to displace all local liturgies that could not be proved to be more than 200 years old. Thus in England it had to take the place of the widespread Sarum Rite. The Pius V Missal was produced in 1570. In the edition of 1604 rubrics were printed for the first time, that is, instructions as to the ceremonies and actions of the priest. The purpose of this was to correct the curious and flamboyant gestures which some priests indulged in. It was quite a momentous change in that this edition of the missal effectively ended the right of the bishops to control the liturgy in their dioceses. The place of the bishops in regulating the liturgy was taken by the new Congregation of Rites, a body set up in Rome for the purpose of answering in the Pope's name all queries as to the implementation of the new Missal and its rubrics.

What were the main differences between the Tridentine Mass and the pre-Trent Mass?

Apart from the standardisation just referred to, there was a pruning of texts run to seed. For instance in the Middle Ages the Gloria had been embellished with pious texts called tropes. These, although popular with choirs, were abolished. Many of the Prefaces also were now abolished, a thing which had happened before. The naming of the Head of State in the Canon was disallowed. Apart from these the Pius V Missal made the rite of Mass which had been approved in Rome in a Missal of 1474 the rite for the whole Latin Church, with the exceptions I have mentioned. Thus it 'Canonised', that is, made an integral part of the Mass many of the mediaeval additions, such as the Elevation, the prayers at the foot of the altar, the Offertory prayers, the signs of the cross in the Canon and the Last Gospel.

Such a far-reaching reform did indeed cure many abuses and so far achieved its purpose. But, as tends to happen with far-reaching reforms, it had consequences which no one had foreseen or intended but which made quite big differences to the Mass as it was actually celebrated. These we must next consider.

The Mass in the 'Ancien Régime'

The Fathers of the Council of Trent set themselves to reform the abuses which were common in the celebration of Mass and we have seen that to this end a standard Missal for the whole Latin rite was made obligatory.

High and Low Masses

The abuses aimed at occurred for the most part in low Masses celebrated by ignorant or careless priests. Hence the stringent controls of the new rubrics as printed envisaged "low" Mass rather than its solemn form. This had the effect of making low Mass the normal form of the Mass, whereas in previous ages the solemn Mass was the norm and low Masses were considered to be making the best of situations when solemn Mass was impossible. The result of this was not only to make solemn Masses less frequent but also that even in solemn Masses the celebrant followed the rubrics of low Mass and had to say to himself silently the parts of the Mass that the other ministers or the choir might be singing. But it must be said that other factors contributed to the decline of solemn Mass. Up till the 14th century Sunday obligation was considered only to be fulfilled by a solemn

Mass. It was considered an abuse that people went to side altar Masses to fulfil their Sunday obligation. But the clergy had so embellished and clericalised the solemn Mass that people were becoming weary of it and the widespread replacing of high Mass with low Mass was popular and filled a need. Another factor, unforeseen by the Council fathers, was that solemn Mass needed clerics and ministers other than priests. Formerly there were always some of these in every town. But now that the training of priests was taken in hand by new seminaries, the only clerics and ministers who could have filled the roles needed for solemn Mass were all in the seminaries and not available for the average church far from a seminary.

The Roman Calendar

Another big change resulting from standardisation was in the area of the feasts of the saints. The Council legislated against the proliferation of saints' feasts and votive Masses and aimed at restoring the calendar for the whole Church to what the Roman calendar had been in the 11th century. But life cannot be controlled so easily. As it was now impossible to touch the actual texts of the Mass, the only way to make any liturgical changes was to introduce new feasts of the saints. The harmony of these new feasts and devotions with the existing calendar involved great subtlety of distinctions and grading which could only be coped with by trained clerics and further widened the gap between the faithful and the liturgy of the Mass. This in turn led to the development of the theatrical, baroque or concert Mass, in which the liturgical texts and actions took second place, while always in strict obedience to the rubrics, and the attention of the faithful was taken up either by the splendours of statuary, painting and architecture, or the beauty of the music. Those who wished to pray had to use prayer books which provided devotions for use at Mass but which scrupulously avoided translating the most important texts, particularly the Canon. It had been no intention of the Council of Trent to conceal the Canon from the faithful, but in the 17th century translations of the Canon were condemned. This seems to have been the result of the state of ecclesiastical politics during the rise of the Jansenist heresy. As the Jansenists were on the whole in favour of educating the faithful and of further reforms in the liturgy, translations of the Canon were made to seem somehow unorthodox and heretical. Thus it was that reform led to situations that needed further reform.

Participation of the Laity

There were other ways however in which the liturgy of the Mass could be affected and which were not problematic. Although the Mass had become more and more something which only the clergy were involved in directly, ways were found of involving the faithful more intimately in the Mass. One of these was Holy Communion and the other was singing. The Tridentine teaching on the Blessed Sacrament increased the reverence for it and also among many devout people the desire to receive it. Both Catholics and Protestants emphasised the horrors of sin and its punishments, which tended to keep people away from Communion. But whereas the Protestant solution to the problem of Christian sin was the doctrine of imputed grace, Catholic saints such as St Philip Neri and St Francis de Sales taught people to come frequently to Communion by going still more frequently to confession and spiritual direction. Teaching of this kind, and the spiritual direction of the Jesuits, made possible the great spiritual revival in 17th century France, Italy, Spain and Germany. But the standardisation of the rubrics of the Mass meant that Holy Communion was normally received after or before Mass, not during it and this was not changed until the time of St Pius X and afterwards.

The other great development in the Mass in the post-Tridentine period was the singing of vernacular hymns during the Mass, which took place mostly in Germany. The purpose of these was to enable the congregation to share in the aims and intentions of the liturgy, an aim common to both Catholic and Protestant pastors and pursued by both with vernacular hymns. These were often used to replace the texts of the Gloria, Sanctus and Agnus Dei as well as in addition to them. This kind of Mass was called in Germany a "*Singmesse*". Many of the efforts to involve the people more actively in the Mass were common to Catholics and Protestants because solutions were being sought for basically the same problem, i.e. that the Mass in the mediaeval period had lost the esteem of most ordinary Christians. It had become complicated and wearisome. People had to be tempted to come to Mass with various bogus promises of temporal benefits. And they did not often go to Communion so that this ceased effectively to be part of the Mass. This general loss of esteem for the Mass, goes far to explain how an attitude of basic hatred and fanatical opposition to the Mass in Protestantism, could take root and not be disapproved of by the people. The Council of Trent helped to restore the dignity of the Mass in the estimation of the Catholic people by means of the reforms which it ordered, but above all by its doctrinal teaching on the Eucharist. It was this teaching, which took as its starting point man's basic need for sacrifice and explained it so clearly, which, together with the shorter form of low Mass, gave such a powerful and distinctive stamp to the "Tridentine Mass".

By means of hymns, spiritual direction and preaching, pastors in the Baroque period sought to make their flocks more familiar with the meaning of the Mass. But many people felt that more needed to be done and in France in the 18th century there was a spate of local developments sponsored by many of the bishops to involve the people in the ceremonies of the Mass. Books were produced by some dioceses resurrecting some of the customs of the pre-Tridentine rites which involved the participation of the people. Enterprising parish priests took great pains to make their Sunday Mass the real centre of life in the village or town. Some of their practises were eventually approved by the highest authority in the Church, as by Pius X in his reform of the Breviary and still more so in our own time by the Second Vatican Council. But at the time these developments were part of the general tendency of the *"Aufklarung"* which later turned against the Church and so caused liturgical developments to be looked at askance by the faithful as well as by Church authority. These developments were known as "Neo-Gallic" because they aimed at reviving some of the ancient, pre-Tridentine, liturgies of the French Church. Among the pundits a debate arose between the Pragmatists, who held that all ceremonies developed from purely practical arrangements, and the Symbolists, who maintained that everything started from symbols and ideas. And then the world erupted, the French Revolution arrived, the end of the "ancien régime" and the establishment of democracy.

To Involve the People

After the time of the French Revolution a different ethos set in which had repercussions on the way Mass was said. In opposition to the Enlightenment, the Romantic Movement in art and literature took place which helped towards a desire to restore Catholicism as it was in the Middle Ages. Growth in scholarship and knowledge of the past led to a desire to revive the rich forms of Mediaeval liturgy. The great figure in this movement was the Benedictine Abbot Gueranger whose publications, zeal and authority fostered an abandonment of Neo-Gallic experimentation and the revival of the ancient Mediaeval texts. Vernacular hymns were out, Gregorian plainsong was in. The aim was still to make the people more appreciative of the liturgy and participate more actively in it, but the means were different. The poetic texts, mystery and symbolism were emphasised and the layman invited to base his prayer life on texts and ceremonies of the liturgy. But it was a liturgy that could only be properly performed in a well-staffed monastery and was not possible in the new towns and vast suburbs of the 19th century world. This programme also only applied to educated and cultured people who could appreciate the beauty of the ancient texts and ceremonies and not be confused and bewildered by the archaic nature and poetic richness. For most people therefore the Mass remained mysterious and unknown and their spiritual needs were satisfied by the growth of a great many devotions and extra-liturgical services, most of which have now died out, but some are still kept alive, like the Stations of the Cross, Benediction and Holy Hours.

The Liturgical Movement

Thus it was that in this century there arose, first of all among the monks and then among priests with pastoral charges, the liturgical movement. Its beginning is usually dated to a conference held at an abbey in Belgium in 1909. Its aims were generally the same as those which had inspired the reforms of the Council of Trent, to enable the people to participate more fully and spiritually in the Mass. Roughly one may divide the liturgical movement into two phases. The first one was to work out what could be changed in the way Mass was celebrated to achieve the above aim, but without any change at all to the texts and rubrics of the Missal. This state prevailed from the beginning of the century until about 1950 when the first reforms of the Holy Week texts and ceremonies were made by Pope Pius XII. The second stage was the changes made in the actual liturgical texts and rites of the Mass.

And so we end this section by a brief account of the changes in the way of using the existing Missal which were undertaken between 1909 and about 1950. I suppose the first reform in this series was that Communion within Mass, rather than after it or quite unconnected with it, was promoted and indeed became more common, as frequent Communion and frequent confession had both gradually been growing since the 17th century. But it shows how retentive people are of ancient habits in liturgical matters, that in the early 60s, Communion was still regularly given before as well as during each early Mass.

Then there was the gradual realisation among liturgically aware Catholics that the normal form of Mass was not low Mass, as had been assumed for practical reasons by the Tridentine reformers, but Solemn Mass. As it was difficult to provide the appropriate ministers required by the rubrics for Solemn Mass in most churches, this realisation led to the development in Germany of the so-called Betsingmesse, like the earlier Singmesse but with the difference that instead of singing hymns the people sang the Ordinary parts of the Mass. The most important change of this period, however, still assumed that low Mass was the norm rather than Solemn Mass. By "norm" here I do not mean most common, but known to be the typical form of Mass, or original form from which low Mass was derived. This development was the Dialogue Mass, in which the people said aloud those parts of the Mass which in a post-Tridentine low Mass were only said by the server. The Dialogue Mass took on quite well and even in England, always slow to adopt continental customs, it had become well-established by the Second Vatican Council.

Now two things are to be noticed about all these changes. First that none of them involved any change in the rubrics or texts and so to adopt them no departure was necessary from the forms established by Church authority, that is no change was necessary in that remarkable phenomenon that only printing had made possible: the uniform and Church-wide standardisation of both texts and ceremonies of the Roman Rite of Mass. Remember it was only printing that made possible the liturgical uniformity desired by the Council of Trent. It is important to be aware that some liturgical developments have their causative factors in matters which have nothing in particular to do with the liturgy.

The second important point to be noticed about this stage of the liturgical movement is also relevant to the next stage, yet to be treated. This is, that it was thought up by the clergy and carried out by them. Obviously this is inevitable in any ecclesiastical event to some extent;

after all they are the professionals and have the duty of attending to these things. But the point is still worth making because it was the result of a trend which had been going on for some time but not for all the Church's history. It was in the Middle Ages that the Roman rite developed many of those features which made the Mass a clerical preserve - the growth of side altars and private Masses, the decline of Communion among the laity, the extinction of the Offertory Procession, the placing of altars against the back walls and the enlargement of sanctuaries. These developments, together with the extra prayers of the Gallica rites, were accepted eventually at Rome and made more necessary a clerical culture which developed alongside and apart from lay culture. This clerical culture was further strengthened after Trent by the establishment of seminaries to train priests. Thus the liturgical movement was a clerical movement, promoted by monks and parish clergy. This feature of a special culture, training and outlook, goes far to explain why the more dramatic changes after the Second Vatican Council, with which we must next deal, came as a shock to many, and a surprise to all of the laity.

The Aims of Vatican II

Now that we have come to the present moment of the story, a slightly different treatment is necessary, seeing that the whole purpose of this booklet is to help us find our bearings after what might be called the liturgical earthquake brought about by the Second Vatican Council. I have therefore two tasks, first to give the reasons why the changes happened in the way they did, second to go through the dozen or so chief changes giving briefly the motives behind them. To do this, I search only among official documents of the Church, not among commentaries and histories reflecting particular, if often justified, points of view by those with axes to grind.

Content and Application

First then, what was the main idea behind the changes and why were they carried out so rapidly and all together, in contrast to what we have usually found to be the case in history that developments in the liturgy have usually happened rather haphazardly and over a considerable period of time? We have seen that the Liturgical movement was started at the beginning of this century by priests and monks in an effort to restore the liturgy as a formative influence and enriching influence in the spiritual life of the faithful. It had become apparent to them that the Mass was for most Catholics, especially those in the new urban centres of population, a mystery whose riches were neither appreciated nor effective.

The first phase of the liturgical movement strove to find ways of making the congregations more involved in the Mass without changing the texts or the rites which had been fixed by the highest authority in the Church. This phase may be said to have culminated in the encyclical *Mediator Dei* of Pope Pius XII in 1947.

The second phase was to change the texts and the rites which could only be done by the highest authority itself, i.e., the Pope and a General Council. As we have seen, both phases are characterised by the fact that they were dominated and carried out by the clergy. I call this process the "Restoration" of the Mass rather than "Reform" in order to distinguish it from the Reform carried out by order of the Council of Trent and St Pius V and also because it contrasts with the procedure of the earlier event in a rather interesting way. In the Middle Ages and the Renaissance period the demand for reform came mainly from the laity, led by the Emperor and the Princes. The clergy were more interested in doctrinal measures against the Protestants, whereas the influential laity was anxious to end the clerical scandals that gave the Protestants their strength. At Trent there was a battle between the Emperor and the Pope as to whether reform or doctrine was to be dealt with and in the end they compromised by alternating the two concerns. At Vatican II it was different. The movement for change came primarily from the clergy anxious to reinvigorate the laity who was making only a feeble resistance to the onset of secularism and materialism. Pius XII saw the liturgical movement in a saying of 1956 as "a providential visitation of the Holy Spirit". He began the second phase, changing the texts, by his reform of the Holy Week rites in 1955. The Second Vatican Council 1962-6 continued this work.

Fruitful Participation

So this brings us at once to the main purposes of the liturgical changes as seen by the Council and the Popes. This was to give greater vigour to the Christian life of the faithful through a full, active and fruitful participation in the liturgy of the Mass. This was to correct what was seen as a passive, dead and distracted way of assisting at Mass. People were missing the spiritual benefits and riches that are contained in the texts and rites of the Mass. This was the same not only for the people but also the priests, most of whom had been taught to regard the liturgy as meaning only a knowledge of rubrics. Pope Paul VI articulated what was felt by many of the clergy when he said that there was a need to re-educate the faithful, purify, and restore dignity, beauty, simplicity and good taste to our ceremonies. This would have effect in a more fruitful and intelligent spiritual life for the faithful, which would make them more resistant to the spiritual dangers of our times. It was becoming clear that the great evils which had produced the Second World War, Fascism and Nazism, had flourished in areas which were to a large extent Catholic. If the faithful had been enriched by their assistance at Mass, if they had had a greater understanding of the meaning of their Christian vocation then surely these pagan revivals would have been very greatly reduced or resisted. The liturgy is a school of Christian life; indeed it is an exacting training for social living, even apart from its supernatural significance.

These convictions in the minds of many prelates and the Pope, help to explain also the haste with which the reforms were put into practice, and also the "industry" of liturgical change which came into being. It was due as Paul VI said to the great desire that "the faithful may no longer be without the anticipated fruits of grace". There was a great sense of urgency, but it was also desired and realised that a great deal of labour was necessary, that the changes were not just to be the result of whims of this or that prelate but the result of careful research and

consideration by many people. Hence the process of
change was carefully organised and carried out. But of
course this could not be without the formation of a
complicated structure of committees, red tape and
consultation. It is impressive to leaf through the
documents and see the minute care given to points raised
and objections made to this or that proposal. The point
was that the need was pressing, delay was harmful but it
must be carefully done, not in an amateurish way.

A distinction was drawn between the divinely
instituted, unchangeable parts of the Mass and the parts
which can and often should be changed with the passage
of time. In our survey of the history we have seen that
although there are hardly any distinct texts or rites that
have not changed at some time or another, there are
certain "constants" in the liturgy which have remained
throughout, ensuring continuity. The Council ordered
that the substance of the Roman rite be preserved when
the rites were revised. It was the prelates' idea, however,
that those parts which can change should change in
whatever ways could promote participation by the
faithful. This meant that while the value of the most
private celebration was to be safeguarded as being truly
an act of Christ and His Church, it was to be made easy
and preferable to celebrate congregationally. To that end
the rites were to be clear and simple, avoiding repetitions

and intelligible enough not to need elaborate explanations. It will be remembered how 19th century liturgists and exponents of the Mass had had recourse to long and detailed commentaries far beyond the capacity of the average Catholic.

The Unity of the Roman Rite

Another important general consideration before the minds of the Pope and his bishops was the need to preserve the unity of the Church in her worship. The changes were made for the Roman rite only, not for any of the other Catholic rites, but it was desired that the whole Roman rite should act as one. To this end the reforms continued the policy inaugurated by Trent, of imposing a standard ritual and not tolerating too much diversity. But in order to provide the needed variety, great numbers of options were introduced into the liturgical texts and elaborate rubrics to ensure the right use of all these options and variables. Unfortunately these rubrics are barely comprehensible and even the conscientious priest feels totally at sea, a fact which partly explains the proliferation of unauthorised experimentation which began as soon as the reforms were announced and which have given the Vatican II liturgy such a bad name among many Catholics. We have seen in history how in the late Middle Ages Rome rather reluctantly ceased to legislate for itself as a local Church and began to take on the role of laying down the liturgical law for all local churches. Consequently the whole Church got into the habit of expecting clear directives on every point even minor ones. But the aim of variety and sensitivity to the needs of congregations of the faithful just could not be fulfilled by obedience to what of necessity became increasingly complicated rubrics which tried to foresee every situation that could arise, every pastoral need. Nevertheless, unity and indeed a certain uniformity remain a need of the Church.

Some of the Modern Changes

Having surveyed the general scene of the liturgical reforms of our time, let us now look at each of the most important changes, to see first the reasons for the change and then to note or recall from the historical record what its previous history was.

Probably the most striking change and the one first brought in was the change from Latin to the vernacular. It was implemented on 7th March 1965. It was felt by Pope Paul VI as a real sacrifice to abandon Latin. The Pope expressed publicly the great loss that the change represented, a real sacrifice deliberately made for the sake of an even greater good. This was a degree of intelligibility which would enable the faithful to participate fully in the Mass. Of course the Mass can never be anything other than a mystery in the theological sense, but the approach to the mystery has never been supposed to be blocked by failure to understand the rites and prayers. The Pope quoted 1 *Corinthians* 14:19 "in church I would rather speak five words which my mind utters, for your instruction, than ten thousand in a strange tongue". For that end he was prepared to lose many cultural and religious values conveyed by the use of Latin and he emphasised that Latin would still be the official language of the Church. Historically, we have seen how Latin replaced Greek in the Roman Mass in the 4th century. At the Council of Trent there was a debate on the question of language and it was agreed that there would be pastoral advantage in the vernacular but it was decided to retain Latin for the time being. Then there were attempts to translate, for the benefit of some mission countries, texts into other traditional "dead" languages but no one liked the result.

High on the list of changes the introduction of "getting up and down all the time". This is a change that priests are perhaps less aware of as irksome but it has been quite a striking change for the faithful in this period. The General Instruction of the Roman Missal directs that the postures of the faithful are important to regulate as a sign of unity, a sign that the faithful form a supernatural unity at Mass rather than just a collection of individuals, but the Missal leaves precise directions to the regional conferences of Bishops. Actually what it gives as a guideline would minimise the "getting up and down" if it was followed. It recommends that the faithful should stand for the opening rites, sit for the readings, and stand for the Gospel, which is what we do. But it recommends that from the Prayer over the Gifts until the end of Mass we should stand except for the brief period of the actual Consecration. However our Conference of Bishops asked for kneeling during the entire Canon, because it reckoned that this had become a traditional custom in these islands and it would disturb people to make a change in it. In the past people mostly stood, as still in Eastern rites, all the time, but in the Middle Ages seating was introduced. A papal master of ceremonies in the early 16th century laid down some directions for the people, prescribing rather more kneeling. Apart from that the Tridentine Missal gave no directions for the people, as it was designed only for the reform of the clergy.

Altars

Altars *versus populum* is one of those changes not mentioned by the Council but which have become almost universal since. The Paul VI Missal of 1969 only orders that when the priest addresses the people, rather than God, in the Mass, he should face them. It also orders that in new churches altars should be free-standing so that Mass can be said from either side. However the new custom began before the Council ended and Cardinal Lercaro, in charge of the Congregation of Rites, had to point out that altars versus populum were not essential for participation, that even with the old arrangement, as at the Oratory, quite a large part of the Mass is still said facing the people and finally that artistic and architectural considerations will often forbid making this change in churches of pronounced architectural character. That said, he gave as the main reason for making the change that it was one way of making participation easier. The fashion came in very soon after the change to the vernacular and the reason is not difficult to see; that once the prayers were being said in the vernacular for the sake of intelligibility, priests considered that it rather diminishes intelligibility not to face people when you are speaking, even if you are not speaking to them but for them. As for the history, we have seen that in early times the altar was surrounded with curtains at the most solemn moments so that the direction of the celebrant's face was of little moment. It was not until the ceremonies of the Mass had become a clerical preserve in the 12th-13th centuries that altars were placed against the wall instead of being free-standing as before. We can see that the question of which way the priest faces could only become important when, as happened in the Renaissance period, all curtains, screens and whatever round the altar disappeared. So this is, really, a new issue for the Church, perhaps a sort of catching up with the general tendency in the Latin rite of Mass to remove barriers between altar and people.

Receiving Holy Communion

Changes in the administration of Holy Communion have taken place in several ways. Some are a continuation of the policy we have already noted as part of the first phase of the liturgical movement to promote frequent Communion, such as the diminution of the fast and the extension of permission for receiving under both kinds. It was also stressed that receiving Communion is the highest form of participation. The reason for Communion under both kinds was that it makes a more striking sign of the "banquet" aspect of the Eucharist, which itself is a sign of its function as an anticipation of Heaven. But other changes have a rather different provenance. Chief among these is the permission to receive Communion in the hand. This was not at all on the agenda of the Council neither does it find a place in the Paul VI Missal although it is in the General Instruction of the Roman Missal. A request by one of the hierarchies in 1969 was considered and turned down by Rome. But a year later it was discovered that hierarchies were already allowing it in some places and it was decided that those who applied for the permission would receive it and England and Wales was one of those that did, so in a way Rome's hand was forced, as it judged that the harm caused by refusing the permission outright would be greater than that caused by allowing it. Recently there are reports of one hierarchy, the Philippines, beginning to ban the practise because people were beginning to treat the Host as just a pious object like a medal or a rosary. At the time of granting the permission it was stated that if rightly taught to the people and so used it can increase one's consciousness of the dignity of being a member of Our Lord's Mystical Body and increase one's faith in the reality of the Body of Christ by allowing it to be touched by hand.

Historically we can see that frequent, weekly, Communion was the rule in the early centuries. The Eucharistic fast seems to have become general in the 4th century. About the 8th century Communion in the hand was being replaced by reception on the tongue, and between then and the 11th century Communion under both kinds and frequent Communion were both dying out. We have seen some of the causes of these developments in earlier chapters.

The introduction of lay people as Extraordinary Ministers maybe should be bracketed with changes in Communion but logically it forms part of another more general change which is the increased use of lay ministers in the celebration of Mass. One of the Council's criteria for active participation was that each person at Mass should do all of but only those parts which belong to them. Thus the ringing of the bell, the singing of antiphons, and the reading of lessons other than the

Gospel should not be done by the priest but by lay ministers. The Council stated that lay people at Mass have a true liturgical ministry. It was stressed that readers should be carefully trained and prepared, that they should wear appropriate dress. However once the principle was admitted, here as in other matters, of precisely worded but usually rather unclear rubrics intended to guide the change into a clerical pattern were ignored by busy priests. Extraordinary ministers of Communion were not envisaged by the Paul VI Missal. Permission for it was given in order to prevent the administration of Communion taking too long and to provide for the shortage of priests. Thus permissions were given in the early 60s for women religious to give Communion and in 1969 the extraordinary ministers were instituted for the same reason. Unforeseen by the legislators was that priests would use the increased permission for Communion under both kinds, which needs more ministers, as an invitation to multiply the numbers of extraordinary ministers, since they see in the latter a means to promote greater participation. Quite recently the point has been made from Rome that the use of extraordinary ministers at a Mass where there are enough priests present to give Communion, even if some priests may be in the congregation and not vested, is not to be done. Looking back into the past, it seems that in early centuries there were indeed many non-priest ministers at Mass, but that these were usually organised into what were called the "minor orders", only two of which remain at this time. It was due to the Tridentine reform that the custom came in of making the celebrant utter every text himself, even when, as at a high Mass, a deacon or some other minister might be reading or singing the text that belonged to him. And we have seen that this development was due to the legislator's point of view that the ordinary priest celebrating a low Mass was the being that had to be tamed, so to speak, in order to eliminate those abuses which the Council had to correct.

The Readings

Returning now to changes which had been ordered by the Council explicitly, we come to the Readings at Mass. The Council ordered that a "more representative portion" of Scripture texts be arranged so as to show the continuity and development of the history of salvation. It was to "stimulate a hunger for God's word" so that the faithful would find in Scripture an "unfailing source of spiritual life, the basis of instruction, and the kernel of theology." Hence we have a three-year cycle for most Sundays. Certain ancient traditions of reading particular books at particular seasons have been retained or revived, such as reading the Acts of the Apostles and St John in Eastertide,

Isaiah in Advent and Christmas time. In ordinary time we
have "semi continuous" readings of each of the other
three Gospels in turn with the Old Testament reading
chosen to fit in with the Gospel and the second reading
semi continuous from the Epistles. An important feature
was the introduction, or rather re-introduction, of the
Psalm after the first reading which it was hoped would
become a feature of the participation of the people, since
it should be sung by them in whole or in part. It was
between the 3rd and 7th centuries that the schemes for the
choice of readings were worked out, before which time
the readings were chosen from whatever texts were
available at the discretion of the celebrant. The Old
Testament reading began to be omitted in the 4th century
and thereafter the multiplication of saints' feasts with
their prescribed readings limited the amount of the Bible
that was actually read at Mass. However the Bible was far
from being neglected; it just passed from the liturgy into
the architecture and stained glass and pictures, all of
which formed a permanent background to the celebration
of Mass. The Church has never felt bound to read a text
on the principle of "that's what it says" but rather has
always exercised freedom in choosing or omitting
passages according to their suitability. At one time
hagiography was permitted at Mass, not being forbidden

until the 8th century, by which time the Canon of Scripture had become fixed for all practical purposes.

The revival of Scripture for Mass and the Psalm was one of those changes which endeavoured to carry out the Council's mandate that "elements which have suffered injury through the accidents of history should be restored to the vigour they had in the days of the holy Fathers", words which were also used by St Pius V in the Encyclical *Quo Primum* of 1570 which established the Tridentine Mass. These words did not indicate "archaeologism" because the elements to be restored were selected according to their relationship to active participation by the faithful.

Bidding Prayers

Another of these ancient elements restored by Vatican II was the Prayer of the Faithful, called in Britain by its mediaeval title of Bidding Prayers. These were intended to be an act of the faithful, an expression of their privilege of "royal priesthood" in which capacity it is their duty to pray for the various needs of the human race at Mass. Historically this is one of the most ancient parts of the Mass, being mentioned as such by St Justin in the 2nd century. It began to change its character slightly in the 5th century when the Canon began to include things formerly mentioned in the Prayer of the Faithful, but it survived into the Middle Ages taking rather more elaborate forms and becoming more of a "prayer of the clergy". The only relic of it permitted by the Tridentine reform was the "*Oremus*" (let us pray) at the beginning of the Offertory. It may have been the intention that this *Oremus* be the introduction of some variable prayers as in the past. In the new Mass it can be seen either as the conclusion to the Liturgy of the Word or as the prelude to the Liturgy of the Eucharist, a sort of link expressing the connection between the two parts.

Eucharistic Prayers

Which brings us to a most important change in the mind of the compilers of the Paul VI Missal, the Eucharistic Prayers or the Canon. The Council had asked that the rite of the Mass be revised and that provided that the substance of the Roman rite was preserved room be made for legitimate adaptation to "different groups, regions and peoples", and if it did not mention specifically the Canon of the Mass, neither did it exclude the Canon from revision. The purpose of the new Canons that are now used is, according to the Missal, to emphasise different aspects of the mystery and the variety of motives for thanksgiving. This would make the Roman Mass less unlike the Eastern liturgies and reflects the liturgical riches discovered since the time of Trent in manuscripts of the past. One Canon would have to be too long if it was to express all the aspects of the Mass and all the things to thank God for. For practical reasons the words of consecration are the same in all the Eucharistic Prayers and the words of consecration of the bread have been added to, to incorporate the expression in Scripture showing the sacrificial nature of Our Lord's Body - "which will be given up for you". The words "The mystery of faith" in the consecration of the Chalice have been moved from that place because they are not among the words spoken by Our Lord.

It was certainly a bold and confident step to make changes in the Canon of the Mass, something no Church which was not confident of its credentials and authority and still believed in the Real Presence would dare to do. Paul VI felt the importance of the event when he spoke of it in 1969 - we have entered "the august, stark, sacred, majestic, awesome sanctuary of the Eucharistic Prayer", the Great Prayer of the Church. We have seen that the Canon of the Mass was nowhere written down till about 300 years had passed and that the Roman Canon was not fixed till about the 6th century and even after that received additions. Unlike the Eastern Eucharistic prayers it allowed no variety except in the Prefaces which came to be considered as not part of the Canon, though in fact in the beginning they formed one prayer with it. Apart from the prefaces, only for a few major feasts were any variable elements present in the Canon.

Sign of Peace

One of the elements from the Mass of the past which the Council wanted restored to the ancient vigour is the Sign of Peace, which is such a noticeable feature of Mass in most churches nowadays. Again, this is intended to be an active participation of the people in which they pray for the peace and the unity of the Church. It is not simply meant to be a social gesture but a gesture of the Church. The Missal leaves it to Bishops' Conferences to decide on whether and how it is to be done, except that the rubric directs the priest to give it to the servers only. It is seen as a preparation for Holy Communion, the idea being that if there is a fellow believer you aren't willing to give or receive the Sign of Peace to or from then you ought to make peace with them before you receive Communion. We have seen in history that at the beginning the Sign of Peace was a formal kiss and that it was performed after the Bidding Prayers and before the Canon (Benedict XVI has given instructions for the Congregation for Divine Worship to investigate whether it should return there). It was moved to its present position in the 6th century among the reforms of the reorganisation of the liturgy of the time of St Gregory the Great. In the Middle Ages it began to die out among the faithful but was retained by the clergy at a high Mass. "*Paxbredes*" (small tablets that were kissed in turn) were used in England for some time. Thus we see that it has never in fact been totally absent from the Roman Mass.

The Liturgical Calendar

Change in the liturgical calendar has been an integral part of the reforms in the Mass of the Roman rite. The Council called for its revision in such a way as to emphasise Sunday as the foundation feast of the calendar, a fact which had been somewhat obscured by saints' feast days which fell on Sundays. The reason for focusing on Sunday was that this is the day on which Mass is most attended, indeed is of obligation and therefore when the faithful can most participate actively. But there is more to it than that, since the reason for Sunday being of obligation is precisely because from the beginning it has been the day of the Mass par excellence. Modern habits of life as well as the ancient tradition that a religious feast begins on the previous evening, accounts for the allowing Sunday Mass to be on Saturday evening. Sunday moreover is the only feast universally acknowledged by all Christians and kept on the same day.

After emphasising Sunday the next most important principle was to emphasise the cycle of feasts of Our Lord as Saviour, which means primarily the Easter cycle with its preparation in Lent and its follow-up to Pentecost. This did not mean extending the cycle evidently, since the Septuagesima Sundays before Lent and the octave after Pentecost were abolished, I suppose because these were thought of as a penumbra of uncertain significance whose removal could enhance the cycle by giving it clear beginning and ending, especially as the character of Lent as a season of preparation for baptism was restored.

While the Christmas cycle remains in the new calendar, the emphasis in the documents concerning the revision is on the Easter or Paschal cycle, as directly celebrating and enabling us to participate in Our Saviour's victory over sin and death and the world and the devil.

As to the Calendar of Saints, there were two main reasons for changes here. One was to prevent the feasts of saints from once more overwhelming the cycle of Our Lord and the Sunday liturgy and the other was to make room in the calendar for the feasts of modern saints and saints from countries which have relatively recently received churches. This is why some previously celebrated saints have been "demoted" to local celebration only and why some whose very existence is doubtful have been expunged.

Historically in the first 200 years the only Christian feasts observed in Rome were Sundays and the Passover which became Easter. In the 4th century Rome began to receive other feast days from the Eastern Churches, her only original contribution being the feast of Christmas which had a great history ahead of it. In subsequent centuries the cult of the saints expanded enormously and expansion continued until the efforts made at retrenchment by the Tridentine reformers, when there was an effort to prune the feasts of the saints by returning to the celebration of the Roman saints as it had been in the 11th century. But such an effort was doomed, since as the Roman rite had now been standardised and fixed the only way to allow any diversity in the liturgy was to invent new feast days.

Sacred Music

The last of this series of striking changes to be accounted for is the music. The Council emphasised the role of music in the Mass, particularly with a view to its ability to foster participation by the faithful. Paul VI stressed it particularly, saying hopefully, "If the faithful sing, they do not leave the Church". The aim was to express the festive, communal, familial character of the liturgy. This being the main aim may account for the enormous growth in "popular" music at Mass since the Council and the tendency to extend music into all public Masses. Indeed it was explicitly stated that ideally every public Mass should have singing in it. But probably they were thinking more of an extension of Gregorian plainchant than the growth of drums and guitars. Nevertheless it was stated that other instruments than the organ could be used, provided they were suitable to the sacred purpose. It was hoped that composers would produce new music suitable for the singing of the liturgical texts by the congregation, particularly for the Responsorial Psalm.

The thinking of the writers of the new Missal was in continuity with the efforts that were made in the 18th century in Germany to have the faithful sing the chants from the Ordinary of the Mass in the vernacular. The preference expressed in the documents for Gregorian chant continues the revival of appreciation of this mode by the liturgical writers of the 19th century and seems to confirm the choice of Gregorian as the archetypical music of the Roman rite. Looking further back into history I understand that what we call Gregorian is a title given to express a continuous development of sacred music going back to the chants of the Temple and perhaps earlier, which, along the course of history, assimilated other currents of music as well, such as the Greek sacred music used in pagan temples. Whether this tradition can assimilate still later modern developments is a question on which one must take expert advice.

Epilogue

This history of the Roman Mass now comes to an end, but its development is not at an end, unless human history is at an end. I cannot really provide a 'happy ending' for the very good reason that we have not yet reached the ending. History goes on. The history of the Mass has shown that problems lead to greater efforts and achievements. We have seen that the development of the liturgy having become a major preoccupation of the universal Church has meant that the pluralism and diversity of earlier times has been abandoned. It has been hoped that by providing the official Missal with many options and variables and choices the needs of different cultures and temperaments can be fully met. But not every Catholic is willing to accept what authority provides. Consequently, right from the beginning of the restoration of the liturgy there has been opposition, dissent and rebellion from both 'left' and 'right'. On the left a proliferation of unauthorised experiments and attempts to overcome the barriers between secular life and liturgy, in which often enough the Mass and the Church simply disappear and one cannot in St Paul's words "recognise the Body". On the right we have the open rebellion against the aims of the Council's intentions for the restoration.

A few comments are necessary about two positive interventions by the Magisterium in recent times. One is Benedict XVI's *Motu Proprio*, *Summorum Pontificum* (2007), which defines the position of the post Vatican II Mass as the Ordinary Roman Rite, and the Mass as it was in 1962 as the Extraordinary Rite. This regularises and makes clear the situation of Old Rite Masses, saying that they are legitimate options in the right circumstances, while at the same time refusing to backtrack completely with regard to the Vatican II Mass. This is an interesting return to a plurality of rites as was seen in earlier periods of the Church's history.

The other intervention is the forthcoming new translation of the Vatican II Rite. This has been prepared partly in response to the many, often justified complaints regarding the currently available English translations. The English translation is of particular importance considering the growing status of English as the universal language of a globalised world. This pamphlet takes a long view, thinking in terms of centuries rather than decades, hence it is worth asking whether in future we are going to see similar changes to those which occurred when the language of the Mass changed from Greek to

Latin, with English being the new major language even in the Church or possibly other world languages, for example, Spanish or even Chinese?

In the history surveyed by this essay we have seen that it is only in relatively recent times that complete standardisation of the Roman Rite has been aimed at and that even then the policy of standardisation was not adopted for its own sake but only to remedy abuses and for pastoral reasons. So it is not necessary to look for uniformity, a uniformity in any case which has never existed even in the Roman Rite. Does this mean that we must prepare for an era of "balkanisation" of the liturgy, with strife and conflict and liturgical "blows and knocks, to prove our worship orthodox"? Maybe. But not necessarily. We should not aim at uniformity but we must absolutely aim at harmony and concord. The orchestra of the praise of God in the Church must be, in obedience to its conductor, the Holy Spirit, in tune and in time and not in discord and cacophony. And so I end, noting only that history tends to show that events that lie in the future are usually surprising and unpredictable.

Sacramentum Caritatis

In this extended reflection on the Eucharist, Pope Benedict underlines the inseparable link between our eucharistic faith and Christian mission. Drawing together the conclusions of his fellow bishops, Benedict calls for a deeper consideration of the inherent mystery, unity, power and vital importance of the identifiable components of the Eucharist we celebrate. Among many salient recommendations, he calls for a carefully prepared liturgy of the word, improved homilies, and Church buildings full of beauty, that echo with music that expresses the faith and love of the people of God. The Eucharist we celebrate and live impacts upon the quality of our Christian life, and so this text is recommended to all.

ISBN: 978 1 86082 453 1

CTS Code: Do 762

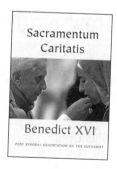

Sacramentum Caritatis

Benedict XVI

POST SYNODAL EXHORTATION ON THE EUCHARIST